CHURTCHED

Tiffani Cabrera

Trilogy Christian Publishers
A Wholly Owned Subsidiary of Trinity Broadcasting Network
2442 Michelle Drive
Tustin, CA 92780

10 9 8 7 6 5 4 3 2 1
Library of Congress Cataloging-in-Publication Data is available.
ISBN 978-1-68556-953-2
ISBN 978-1-68556-954-9 (ebook)

CHURTCHED

-THE STATE OF BEING NEGATIVELY INFLUENCED BY A CHURCH EXPERIENCE THAT HURTS/HINDERS THE GROWTH OF YOUR RELATIONSHIP WITH CHRIST

-THE STATE OF BEING TURNED OFF BY GOD DUE TO A NEGATIVE CHURCH EXPERIENCE

-THE STATE OF BEING LEARNED IN THE CHURCH CULTURE, BUT IGNORANT IN THE THINGS OF GOD

DEDICATION

This book is dedicated to any and everyone who loves the Lord and has had heartbreak due to a negative church experience. I pray this book leads you into healing and understanding. In sharing this experience, I pray you realize that you are not alone, and this too shall pass!

> For our light and momentary troubles are achieving for us an eternal glory that far outweighs them all. So we fix our eyes not on what is seen, but on what is unseen, since what is seen is temporary, but what is unseen is eternal.

> 2 Corinthians 4:17-18 (NIV)

ACKNOWLEDGEMENTS

Throughout this journey, God placed mentors in my life to support, educate, develop, and guide me. Both stood in the gap and prayed for me and my family during a difficult season. I thank and appreciate them.

Shakir Ministries

I credit Shakir Ministries for assisting me in my spiritual development. I was dissatisfied with my level of knowledge and understanding, so I began taking classes through their online Ministry School, F.B.I. (Founded Believers Institute). I completed several courses: Supernatural, Warfare and Deliverance, Prophetic, and HELPS. Each course strengthened my Godly foundation, helped me see more clearly and navigate a lot of the things I was experiencing.

shakirminstries.org
thefoundedworld.org (FBI Course)

DREEMM Team Cincinnati, OH

*(Deliverance Restoration Education Empowerment for Me Ministries)

This journey left my family and I scarred. Apostle Edwards and her DREEMM Team have continuously provided support, prayer and education while leading us through deliverance.

dreemm.org

TABLE OF CONTENTS

FOREWORD

One of the most dangerous things that a Christian can face is friendly fire. Satan does not need to attack the body of Christ head-on, sometimes, he just needs to infiltrate what's already existing and attempt to kill them from the inside out.

The Bible talks about how "you make the word of God of no effect through your traditions....and you do several things like this" (Mark 7:13, NKJV). Jesus was basically saying that you do more harm to the word of God through your man-made traditions and practices. Sadly, these practices have become the norm for some of our modern-day churches.

I have known Tiffani and her family for some years now. When I first met her, she was in the middle of some of the situations she has described in this book. I can remember walking her through some of the landmines and helping her to see God's perspective as it relates to the situation. Since then, I have discovered her to be a dedicated mother, wife, and Christian woman.

It broke my heart to hear some of the encounters she faced, which she described within pages of this book. I was fortunate enough to share my experiences, as well as some of my teaching with her to help assist. Some of these teachings that she referenced were about the "Seducing Spirit" and the "Spirit of Religion." I had no idea how much of an impact it would have on her life and her ministry. The Bible says that "iron sharpens iron, so one man sharpens another" (Proverbs 27:17, AMP). Simply, two of the same kind can only make it better once they connect and start to share with each other. I have experienced a similar hurt from the religious community as I was developing in ministry.

My prayer is that you can read this book and walk away better instead of bitter. Satan's objective is to steal, kill, and destroy (John 10:10, NIV). That can mean that if he's stealing your relationship with God, killing your relationship with God, or destroying your relationship with God, he has completed his work. Unfortunately, that destruction can sometimes come through members of the body of Christ inside our local churches.

I'm sure you would agree that there is no such thing as a "perfect church," because if so, none of us would be a part of it. However, I think you may also agree that when you come to the house of God, you and your family expect the leadership to be trustworthy with your vulnerability. You should rightly assume that they can help you in areas that you struggle with. I don't believe that this is the wrong approach; you should be able to open up to those you trust.

Satan has caused so much hurt in the body of Christ that the people are reluctant to trust their leaders, and they have trouble opening up because they're not sure if it's safe. I believe the church is a place of healing for broken people. I believe the church is a place of restoration for God's people who are weary from the journey.

At the darkest moment of Jesus' life, he turned to his disciples and commanded them to "watch and pray" (Matthew 26:41, NIV). He said this because he knew his time was at hand, and that Satan (through people) would be coming for the church at any moment.

That command prompts the modern day disciples to watch the culture, or in this case, watch what's going on in our local churches and pray about specific situations. We should allow the Holy Spirit to open our eyes to see what the enemy is doing behind the scenes and prepare for what's coming next.

I truly believe that the days are over of just simply joining a church because your family goes there. We truly must be sensitive to the Holy Spirit to attend the places of worship where the Holy Spirit guides and directs us. As you read this book, I pray that "your eyes of understanding will be enlightened" (Ephesians 1:18, NKJV) and that you will obtain that "good and perfect will" (Romans 12:3, NIV) of God as it relates to serving in your local church and submitting yourself to Godly leadership.

Pastor Lawrence Shakir
The Foundation of the World Church
F.B.I. (Founded Believers Institute)

This book is the result of a year-end fast at the conclusion of a difficult season. It was titled and written completely by the Holy Spirit. Thank you, Holy Spirit!

Mature Christians Only

This book was not written to bash the church. If you're looking for a reason to justify any misdirected church hurt in your heart that has turned into bitterness and hate, you won't find it here. The things we experienced are not unique to our family or this church. It is something that has been affecting the church for centuries. The devil is crafty and has found a way to use the church as a vehicle to water down the Gospel. He's cunning, and we have been deceived. I am sharing this story to help unveil some of his tricks. The goal is to witness, educate, and bring healing.

I love the Lord with all my heart, and all his people, including the church referenced in this book. We have forgiven, and we keep them in prayer. We must remember that the battle isn't against flesh and blood, but against spiritual wickedness in high places (Ephesians 6:12-13, KJV). Everything that we experienced was due to spirits and open doors within ourselves. Demons will continue to enter a home that has been swept clean if it's not filled with the Holy Spirit (Luke 11:24-26, NIV). Remember that.

INTRODUCTION

The following is a testimony detailing an eye-opening experience my family and I endured with the first church we truly committed ourselves to. It is a front row seat to the hardships we faced, the effect it had on our family dynamic, our walk with the Lord, and how even still, God gets the glory.

SPIRIT FILLED

I remember being filled with the Holy Spirit for the first time at age 16.

My parents flew me to Atlanta to spend Christmas with my aunt and uncle. We went to church one Sunday, and the pastor did an altar call asking if anyone wanted to be baptized in the Holy Spirit. At that time, I had no idea what that meant (I didn't grow up in church). My uncle invited me to go up to the altar with him, and I accepted (what could it hurt?).

I stood in a long line of people who were waiting for the pastor to touch them on the forehead. I noticed how everyone seemed to fall back at the touch of the pastor's hand. Was that protocol? I'd never seen anything like that before. As I got closer to the front, I wondered if I should fall back or not. I mean, I didn't want to look out of place.

Eventually, I started having a funny feeling throughout my body. I felt a pull. It was like electricity. I felt light, and my stomach was stirring. The closer I got to the front of the line, the stronger it got!

"What is this???" I thought.

I remember telling my uncle that I felt weird.

He simply said, "It's the Holy Spirit baby!"

Before I knew it, I was in the front of the line. I walked up to the pastor and turned to face him. The only thing I remember is, "something, something, something, in Jesus' name!". He put his hand on my forehead, and I dropped! No prompting. No rehearsal. It was real!!!

I didn't know it but receiving the Holy Spirit that day would be key in saving my life and the life of my future family.

FAST FORWARD

I didn't have another encounter with the Holy Spirit until about 20 years later. I'd graduated high school, went to the military, got out of the military, got married, had a child, got divorced, got remarried, and had another child. During those years, I rarely attended church, if ever. Jesus was the last thing on my mind.

Having reached a certain level of maturity (which wasn't all that mature), my husband and I decided that we wanted the Lord in our lives. We wanted a better future. We wanted better for our marriage, kids, and family.

A friend of my husband had been inviting us to church. After a few invitations we accepted. The church service was amazing! The pastor was funny, down to earth, and made the Bible easy to understand. We also enjoyed the choir. My husband and I agreed that we'd found our new church home. Within two weeks, we were members.

I was happy, my husband was happy, the kids were happy, life was good...for now.

Things started happening, and I wouldn't figure out why until a couple of years later.

I DON'T LOVE GOD

A few months in, my husband and I began serving in the ministry. Leadership immediately stated seeing a pastoral call on my husband's life. They encouraged him to serve in a few areas and to begin taking classes on the Ministerial track. My husband had been dealing with a life-long struggle with purpose, identity, and self-worth. For the first time in his life, he began feeling worthy. The recognition and attention were unknowingly filling the void within him.

I also began to serve. I really enjoyed it.

The kids liked going to church and seemed happy with the children and teen ministries. Everything was good...except for something strange going on with our daughter.

She told us that she had started hearing voices telling her that "she doesn't love God." She expressed how it made her upset because she knew it wasn't true. She'd also began telling us that she knew how to fly. She described being in her room, and her body physically lifting off the ground. None of this had never happened before. My husband and I knew that something wasn't right.

We talked to one of the pastors and was referred to someone in the church who had experience in counseling children. She spoke to our daughter, and she guided and instructed us on how to pray over her. We did what was instructed, and eventually the voices and flying stopped.

DEPRESSION

About six months in, I noticed a change in me. I continued to serve in the church faithfully, but I felt like I was slowly dying inside.

I had no energy. I had no desire to go to work. Everyday tasks (cooking, cleaning etc.) were agony. It was extremely difficult for me to function as a mother and wife. I would get home from work, cook and lay down. I had no joy. I was depressed.

To make matters worse, I was diagnosed with a kidney disease called PKD (Polycystic Kidney Disease) that has no known cure. This disease causes multiple cysts on both kidneys (and sometimes the liver), and somehow increases the risk of brain aneurysms. It has the potential to hinder kidney function and lead to failure. It's progressive in nature, so it usually worsens over time. The cysts in my kidneys didn't resemble the typical PKD cysts. They were what's called complex cysts.

The doctor suspected that they were cancerous. Because of the location of the cysts, they were unable to biopsy without damaging one or both kidneys (kidney tissue doesn't regenerate as well as other organs), a risk they didn't feel was worth taking. The plan was to just continue to monitor them.

I felt helpless and didn't think I'd be alive in five years. In addition to the depression, I was now struggling with fear of death and self-pity.

I felt so alone.

My husband was physically and emotionally unavailable. He had started training for boxing 5-6 days a week and was serving in several ministries at church. I poured my heart out to him and told him about my depression and fear of death. He seemed like he cared at that moment but went back to being distracted with all his activities. I would later find out that he was fighting demons of his own.

I slipped deeper into depression. I developed an obsession with the thought of my death that eventually turned into suicidal ideation. When I would go to the doctor for my routine MRIs, I would secretly hope that the results showed a progression of my disease.

This level of depression lasted for about a year. My mind was completely twisted, but I was still serving faithfully in the church.

One day, the church brought in a guest speaker who taught on the meaning of true worship. I learned that we are to worship the Lord with our lives and not just in song. It sparked something inside of me. I figured that if I was going to die soon, I needed to make sure I was right with our Lord Jesus. I needed to give my family the best years of my life. I needed to grow closer to Him and lead my family closer to Him. I knew that if I died, my family was going to need Jesus more than ever.

I was done with this depression and decided to act.

I knew that to get closer to God, I had to lead a life of worship to Him like I'd learned. I decided to go on an indefinite consecration, even though at the time, I didn't even know what that meant.

I ceased all things that did not feed my spirit. I rarely watched TV. If I did, it was educational, biblical, or family-friendly. I cut out all secular music and only listened to Christian music. During idle time, I read Christian books and played Christian games. I limited my interaction with people who didn't help build up my faith. I quit all social media. I used my phone primarily for making phone calls, and I stayed off the internet unless absolutely necessary. About six months later, I woke up one morning feeling delivered. The cloud of depression was gone!

Shortly after my deliverance, I received the gift of tongues. I didn't ask for it and wasn't expecting it. I went up to the altar for prayer. An intercessor prayed over me and laid hands on me. The fire of the Holy Spirit overwhelmed me, and I started stuttering.

Initially I had no idea what was happening, but I later realized it was the beginning of tongues. Shortly after that experience I started having prophetic dreams. Just like the tongues, I didn't know what they were. I would see numbers and times. I heard names, sounds, heavenly songs, scripture, and phrases. I saw images of things to come, and images that provided warning. All of this was new to me, and I didn't realize that it would help bring clarity in the future.

ABANDONMENT

As I mentioned earlier, my husband was fighting demons of his own. As a child, he never felt good enough. He felt invisible and had a low self-worth. The issues were never resolved, so he developed a negative self-image.

Unfortunately, all of the mindsets carried over into adulthood.

I also mentioned that the day we stepped into the church, leadership stated seeing a pastoral call on my husband's life. They immediately started encouraging him to take ministerial classes. They often called him out during services and altar calls, referencing the call on his life. Many hands were laid upon him, and many words were spoken. Leadership and the whole congregation were rooting for my husband to walk in what they recognized as the calling on his life. He was encouraged to serve in various areas in the ministry.

For the first time, my husband was starting to feel like he had a purpose. He'd struggled with purpose his whole life, and this experience was filling the void.

As time passed, he did as was suggested. At one point in time, he was serving in five different areas! He felt as if he was on top of the world. He was finally involved in something that had meaning. He no longer felt invisible.

In addition to ministry, he had started training for boxing. As a child, he'd always loved watching it with his dad. As an adult it turned into a passion. He'd struggled with his weight for many years, so when the opportunity to train presented itself, I encouraged him to go for it.

He trained for 5 to 6 days a week and quickly began dropping weight. He was highly dedicated and enjoyed the fruit of his labor. He'd eventually drop almost 100lb. He was on top of the world.

He was the man at church, the man in the gym, and I'd later find out that he was the man at work as well.

All of this sounded good, but there was one major problem. He was working on being great for the church and in his physical health but was neglecting his first ministry: home.

The kids and I weren't seeing this great man of God who had lost a ton of weight. We were seeing a man who had abandoned his family. It was hard for us to celebrate his accomplishments. The kids expressed how they missed him and how he was doing too much. During this time, I was still in a season of depression (as mentioned in the last chapter), and this broke my heart. I poured my heart out to him and told him how badly the kids, and I missed him. I told him how I thought I was going to die soon and confessed that I was battling the fear of death. He seemed touched for a moment, but in his response, he stated how he was only serving God and being obedient to his calling.

This broke my heart even further. He just didn't get it. He was working so hard to be a pastor but wasn't seeking the Lord. He wasn't praying, fasting (on his own), or reading the Word. He was neglecting Jesus and his first ministry. He had become very prideful and self-centered. All the attention and praise he was receiving from the church was feeding his ego. The kids and I could not rec-

28

ognize him. He was a different person.

This behavior lasted for about two years. Our marriage and our family were slowly being destroyed.

I'd hit my breaking point. This is the point in time where I began my 6-month consecration. I knew that I couldn't control my husband's actions. I knew that I needed to draw near to the Lord. I knew he was the only one who could heal me and allow me to help lead my family to Him.

As mentioned in the last chapter, at the end of the consecration, I woke up delivered. The cloud of depression and heaviness lifted.

Thank God for his timing because a week or two later, my husband admitted to acting inappropriately with women at his job.

My heart was broken, and my mind was blown!

Angrily I called him a liar and a fake. I didn't understand how he could act so holy and put together in front of church folks but be a complete mess at home and a lustful adulterer at work? How could his conscience allow him to lead this double life? How can a man who was working so hard to become a pastor engage in this adulterous behavior? He admitted to behaving this way for more than a year. Why didn't he realize it was wrong? We worked for the same employer and knew the same people why wasn't he worried that I'd find out? Did he even care? Where was the conviction?

Suddenly, I had a moment of clarity: my husband didn't have a relationship with Jesus.

He had been too busy pursuing the calling and the physique of his dreams. He was chasing everything but Jesus.

After many painful discussions, my husband realized that it was best for him to fall back from all the commitments to the church and boxing. He was broken and was in fear of losing his marriage and family.

He informed the church that he would be stepping back.

THE VEIL LIFTED

We immediately began working on our marriage and family. We had many heartfelt conversations and began to get to the root of his behavior. We uncovered major trauma and events from his past that shed light on the current situation. These events scarred him and contaminated his identity and self-worth. He admitted having battled with these things since early childhood. He was in pain.

At that moment, I realized that though he had done wrong, he needed my support more than ever. We agreed that we needed help navigating this.

We began attending counseling sessions with one of the pastors from church. It was awkward for me because before this, the pastor and I had never had a real conversation. My husband was better acquainted, so he started off by explaining why we were there. I could tell the pastor was a bit shocked.

As the session progressed, I started feeling more comfortable. We were given a chance to express ourselves equally, which made me feel valued. I cried and described the betrayal and shame I was feeling. It felt good to let it out. By the end of the session, I was back to feeling awkward.

The pastor asked us who knew about the incident and advised us not to tell anyone else. The explanation was, "it wouldn't be wise given the direction he's going in ministry." In other words, let's keep it a secret so that his reputation and the plans you have for him won't be ruined.

I understood and agreed that it wasn't wise to involve several people in this private matter, but I didn't agree with the underlying motive. It bothered me because I knew that the motive wasn't pure. The concern had nothing to do with our marriage. We were there for support for our marriage, but the concern was for the ministry.

I found it disturbing.

I did what was advised, but not for the reason the pastor stated. I knew that the condition of our marriage was delicate, and that involving too many people could hinder the healing process. I wanted our healing more than anything.

One evening, a few days after the initial session, my husband admitted to me that he hadn't disclosed the whole truth regarding the behavior at work. He shared additional details that revealed how far off into the deep end he had gone. These details broke my heart even further. I couldn't understand why he didn't just tell me the whole truth from the beginning.

In church that Sunday, he went up to the altar for prayer. The pastor approached him. He immediately fell to the floor and started bawling. I watched in shock because I'd never seen him break down like that. When we got home, I referenced his breakdown and asked if he was okay. He admitted that he broke down because he felt guilty about lying to the pastor about his activities at work during our first session. I was stunned. When he confessed those things to me, he didn't bat an eye or shed a tear.

Why did it seem like his heart had more allegiance to the pastor than to me? It was so unsettling to me I had to question him. He immediately got defensive. What in the world was going on?

We had a couple more sessions with the pastor. I don't recall everything that was discussed, but I do remember boundaries, accountability, and rebuilding the relationship. We were given guidelines that would help us to do so.

We set up accountability. This consisted of sharing passwords to all personal accounts and removing locks from phones. We also established boundaries. We agreed to include each other in communications with the opposite sex, not to allow any unnecessary physical contact (i.e., church hugs), and not to provide transportation without the other spouse present. In an effort to rebuild the relationship, we also started dating again. We went once or twice a week. We went to breakfast, lunch, dinner, and movies. Sometimes, we would simply meet up for coffee. We were committed. We were also intentional about spending more quality time with the kids. We did movie nights and game nights. The kids were confused by the sudden togetherness, but they went with it.

My husband had also started focusing on building his relationship with God. He began praying, worshipping, and reading the Word.

Everything seemed to be going in the right direction...until it wasn't.

Though my husband stepped back, we were still attending Sunday service. Before we knew it, leadership and staff began nudging him to start serving again. It was said that they were concerned about him staying away for too long. I was bothered by the gesture because no one had asked how we were doing as a family. Not everyone knew the details behind his break, but everyone knew that he'd stepped back to work on family. My husband had made that clear.

I also found it odd that the pastor that provided council never checked in with us to see how we were doing. The concern only seemed to be about my husband serving again. If I were a pastor and had a leader in training fall into adultery, I would want to check up on them to see how they're doing. That wasn't the case here.

I'd also started noticing instances where my husband and I would enter a room together, and only my husband would be acknowledged. There were times when we would be standing right next to each other, and they would greet my husband and not me.

One Sunday, we were sitting behind one of the pastors. After service ended, the pastor turned around and said to my husband, "Nice to see you, man of God." I was standing right next to him, but not a word was spoken to me.

Why was this happening?? I knew what I was seeing, but it didn't make sense! I was in disbelief.

One day during a leadership teaching I was sitting next to my husband, as usual. I was looking at the pastor as the sermon was being delivered. I was cold, so I grabbed my husband's arm to cuddle closer to him. As I was doing that, the pastor happened to look directly at me. We locked eyes. The gaze probably only lasted a moment, but it seemed unusually long and awkward.

The pastor quickly looked away and said, "You know what else God told me? Some of you are too yoked to our husbands."

What????!!!! Was that a jab at me? The timing of the statement was eerie. It seemed out of the blue! Was I reading too much into it? Did I imagine it?

Over the next few days, I tried to forget about it. I couldn't stop thinking about it. I needed to make sure I hadn't imagined it. I went online and found the recording. I fast-forwarded to the moment in question. Sure-enough, it clearly showed the pastor pausing in the middle of the teaching, holding a gaze in our direction, and making the statement.

Part of me was relieved because I was beginning to feel like I was crazy. The other part of me was hurt and confused. To anyone else, it may have seemed minor, but I knew in my heart there was more to it.

What was the motive behind the statement? What did it mean? What was up with this church??

As mentioned earlier, my husband was working on his relationship with God. He was praying, worshipping and reading the Word consistently. He quickly began to grow frustrated and weary because he didn't feel like he was getting the "results" he expected. He still wasn't discerning the voice God and still didn't see the fruit of the Holy Spirit in his life as he desired. He'd been to the altar many times and pleaded with God in his prayer closet for a fresh, tangible filling.

I explained to him that growing in relationship with God takes time, cannot be rushed, and must grow organically. I explained to him that it takes as long as it takes. He did not like that and expressed feeling as if he should be "further" along. He felt like a failure because he had been prepping to be a pastor for almost two years but didn't know the Lord. In his mind, too much time had been wasted, and it was up to him to make it up. He had a schedule in his head and was attempting to have relationship with God and be Spirit-filled within a certain time frame.

I tried to explain to him that God doesn't work like that. I reminded him that Jesus is the foundation of ministry, not the other way around. He seemed annoyed and angry with me though I was only speaking the truth. He just couldn't receive it.

Lord, help!

None of this was adding up. My husband was chasing ministry harder than he was chasing Jesus. The church was tugging at him and didn't seem to value the time he was taking to work on his family. They didn't seem to care about his spiritual growth. No one checked on his foundation with Jesus. Given the fleshly things that almost destroyed our marriage, I thought that at least the pastor that counseled us would feel it important to check in on his progress. I was wrong.

This was not making any natural sense!

I also started noticing how the church wasn't growing. People visited and didn't stay. A large portion of the congregation was on staff on Sundays. It reminded me of the kids' show from the 90's, "Saved by the Bell," where the same five students made up every club and every team on the show. They were the cheer squad, football team, choir, and student council. I found it hilarious. I never thought I would see it in a church.

How were we reaching the lost?

The same people were repeatedly going to the altar. It didn't seem like there was victory. I didn't judge them, but I wondered if there was any effort toward healing being made outside of Sunday service. It seemed like they had more trust and hope in the pastors than they did in Jesus. Altar calls were made, and the pastors routinely called individuals up by name to receive prayer (usually the same people). My husband was singled out on various occasions. As indicated earlier, he received many laying on of hands and many prayers. Many "prophesies" were spoken over him regarding the call on his life.

One day during a meeting, one of the pastors discussed all the positions in the church that needed to be filled. I looked at the positions and knew that we didn't have leaders to fill them. I had heard that other families within the church were also having issues and knew first-hand how hard it is to lead when your house isn't in order. Out of maturity and a genuine desire to help, I offered insight and a suggestion. I told leadership that I believed the empty positions were connected to the family issues within the church. I asked if the church could provide ongoing training and guidance to assist families in balancing ministry and home.

One of the pastors answered by saying, "God knew you had a family when he called you."

What???? That was not an answer. I asked a genuine heart-felt question, and that was the reaction? From a pastor? I didn't deserve that.

Marriage and family were the first institutions God created, and the Bible clearly mentions how church leaders needed to manage their households well. He loves and values family! So should a church! So should a pastor! This couldn't be real!

With everything that had been going on, I went to the altar one day very broken. I was praying in the Spirit and crying heavily. I was broken before the Lord.

One of the pastors came up to me and said, "Stop being so arrogant," and moved on to the next person. There was no elaboration or explanation. They just dropped the bomb and kept it moving. I know that sometimes God has concise words for his children, but where was the strengthening, encouragement, and comfort? I couldn't wrap my head around it. Why would a pastor deliver a word in that manner to someone who is broken before the Lord? I was crushed.

After that day I vowed never to go the altar again.

I began feeling like I was being personally attacked. What did leadership have against me? I served faithfully, and I truly loved the Lord. I fasted, prayed, worshipped, and read the Word regularly. I had genuine relationship with the Lord. Couldn't they discern that? Did they even care? Isn't this the type of person that is valuable in ministry?

I was beginning to feel invisible and less than. It was becoming clear that all they cared about was getting my husband to the pulpit.

I was in turmoil. I doubted myself because I didn't grow up in church. I thought to myself, "I've only been on this walk for a few years, and these people have been walking for decades. How can they not see what I'm seeing? Am I seeing correctly? Is there something wrong with me?" I had these thoughts often. I didn't feel qualified to speak up, nor did I feel like anyone would care.

Though there were many red flags, we still attended the church. My husband was still on his break and battling feelings of inadequacy. The tugs from leadership continued, and his self-esteem declined. He started to express that staying home didn't feel purposeful. My feelings were hurt because it made me feel like he valued ministry more than his family. We were still very broken. It felt like we were a house divided. Our marriage was still damaged, and my husband's relationship with our kids still needed major work.

Wasn't this important to him? Why did the needs of the church hold more weight than the needs of our family? What happened to my husband?

Something was terribly wrong. The veil was lifting. I started praying and fasting. I needed revelation from the Holy Spirit. I knew this was much bigger than me, my husband, my family, and the church.

For the next couple of months, I prayed, observed, and listened. I prayed for my spiritual eyes and ears to be sharpened. I observed how leadership and staff seemed to worship my husband. I listened to the jabs from the pulpit indicating that family can sometimes get in the way of God's calling in one's life. This happened on a few occasions. I observed as the pulls for my husband to return to ministry continued. I listened to my husband's inner turmoil regarding the whole situation. Eventually the pressure from the pulling worked.

It was suggested that my husband take a prayer class. He agreed.

I remember being in the room for the first prayer class. It was a one-on-one Zoom call with one of the pastors. I overheard my husband telling the pastor how he didn't feel comfortable leading in certain positions in the church because he wasn't sure if he was filled with the Holy Spirit (due to the lack of fruit) and didn't feel led by Him. He expressed how he was still unable to decipher God's voice in his life, and that he was tired of always relying on other people to hear a Word from God. I wondered what this had to do with prayer and how the conversation got to this point, but I continued to listen. I was curious to see how the pastor would respond.

Instead of validating my husband's concerns and providing wise counsel, the pastor basically encouraged him not to be concerned with the things he mentioned and to move forward anyway. No advice was given on how to recognize God's voice, strengthen relationship with the Lord, or to walk in the Spirit as my husband so desired.

My mind was blown! What was the rush??? He desired to seek first the Kingdom as the Word says. Why was this being disregarded? Relationship comes before ministry!!

Just when I thought the meeting couldn't get any worse, I overheard the pastor telling my husband how "sometimes, family can get in the way of your calling."

There it was!! This confirmed that the jabs from the pulpit were directed toward us.

I don't know why we continued to attend the church, but we did. The following Sunday, without fail, came another jab. During the sermon, the same pastor said, "some of ya'll just HAVE to hear God for yourselves. In the Old Testament God spoke through prophets all the time." The Biblical reference was correct, but the motive behind the statement wasn't pure. I knew the statement was in response to the conversation the pastor had with my husband where he expressed the desire to hear God for himself. What a bold move! My spirit was completely vexed! Something ungodly was in operation, but I still couldn't put my finger on it. My husband's eyes starting to open to what was happening, but the dedication to the church was still blinding him.

I continued to fast, pray, and read the Word. I needed more clarity. Attending church had become very unsettling for me. The check in my spirit was stronger than it had ever been. I felt like I was slowly dying inside. My husband was conflicted and confused. Our family healing process had come to a halt. I prayed for God to give me a clear revelation and an undeniable release from the church.

Eventually, the last straw was placed on the camel's back. It happened at the end of service during an altar call.

I was at the front of the sanctuary serving. My husband was sitting in the congregation with our children. One of the pastors singled him out (as usual) and says, "I don't know what happened with you or what you did. You have fallen back from the ministry. You have been gone long enough. Start taking classes or do what you have to do. I know family is important...BUT the church needs you."

Did I hear correctly?

"Family is important, but the church needs you."

The check in my spirit was so strong it felt like an uppercut to my gut. How can a word like that come from the pulpit?? How can the pastor dismiss me and the kids right in front of us and in the presence of the whole church?

"The church needs you?" Christians aren't supposed to die to self for the church, we die to self for Jesus! This was NOT the Holy Spirit speaking! I felt physically ill. This feeling lasted for days.

God gave me the impression that we were not safe in that church, and that we needed to leave. I expressed my concern with my husband and shared what I had received from God. He appeared to empathize and agreed with my concerns, but I sensed that his allegiance was still to the church. He had received the word that was spoken over him that day. He felt condemned and like a failure. He expressed feeling as if backing from the ministry was an act of disobedience to God. He was so conflicted. He told me he didn't feel capable of "doing family and ministry at the same time" and wasn't sure we were supposed to leave the church. He hadn't received the word from God for himself.

I was very hurt and frustrated, but I understood that though he didn't have eyes to see or ears to hear, he was the natural head of the household. I knew that the word I received from God to leave the church was urgent, but I had to allow my Husband to reach the conclusion on his own. I didn't want him to resent me in the future. I prayed for wisdom and came up with a compromise. I asked my husband if we could take two months away from the church completely. I explained that it would allow us time to pray, fast, hear from God and conclude without influence or pressure from the church. He agreed.

Hallelujah!

REVELATION

We informed church leadership and immediately started our break. The immediate focus was on our marriage and family. We knew we needed further assistance, so we started both couple and individual therapy. While in expectation, we waited and listened for a word from God. I mentally recapped everything that we'd experienced and witnessed:

1. Our daughter hearing demonic voices and possibly levitating

2. The worst depression of my life and wishing death upon myself

3. My husband committing adulterous acts (putting his job and marriage at risk) while being groomed to be a pastor

4. My husband abandoning his family

5. Church leadership worshipping him while mistreating me

6. The disregard for family

7. The push for my husband to be a pastor without being properly discipled

8. The lack of deliverance in the church house

9. The halt in church growth.

I prayed and meditated on the Word. As the days passed, I kept hearing the name of a seducing spirit (Note: The main goal of a seducing spirit is to lure you away from the will of God. It may seem like God, but it is of the devil. It generates false signs and wonders. It draws people away according to their own lust. It causes deception and a straying from the truth.) I initially thought it was a coincidence, but I soon realized it was a word from the Lord. I stumbled on it while reading the Bible, heard it in conversations, in sermons and on a Christian talk show.

On the show, a woman shared how she and her husband attended a church that had this seducing spirit in operation, and how she almost died. The spirit was cursing her and making her sick. The spirit wanted her husband!!! That immediately sent chills down my spine.

Could this be what we'd been dealing with?

God had already put the check in my spirit and informed me that we weren't safe there. I'm not accusing the church of attempted murder because we wrestle not with flesh and blood. I do believe the spirit was in operation at the church and attempted to kill my spirit, so that I would surrender to the spirits of suicide and premature death. When that didn't work, it tried to destroy our marriage. When that didn't work, it tried to divide and conquer by seducing my husband away from his family. The spirit caused so much confusion in my husband's head that he had no idea what relationship to the Father was.

In the natural, it appeared that he was being groomed for ministry, but in the spirit, he was being adopted by a spirit of religion. It seduced him into worshipping the calling and not the one who calls. "They exchanged the truth about God for a lie and worshiped and served created things rather than the Creator-who is forever praised. Amen" (Romans 1:25, NIV). The door was opened, and in came error, deceit, pride, and lust.

Wow!!!

I thanked God for the revelation and shared it with my husband.

Because he was still having trouble hearing God's voice for himself, he was reluctant to receive what I was telling him. He said that he'd feel bad if we just left the church without talking to them and giving them a chance to change. I expressed understanding and agreed that we should at least talk to them. It was the mature thing to do.

My husband and I sent a text to a few of the pastors and asked if we could meet with them as soon as possible regarding some things we had observed in the church. They agreed.

For the next few days, I prayed and asked God for the words. I started writing things down. I shared them with my Husband. We discussed and agreed on what was written. He suggested that I read it to them since most of it was about the things I'd observed and experienced. He said that he would make it clear to them that he was in agreement with everything in the letter.

We met with leadership a couple of days later. We were extremely nervous, but we knew it was necessary. My husband started off by thanking them for taking the time to talk to us. He explained that he agreed with everything in the letter, and that he hoped it would shed light on things that may have been overlooked. He explained that we were sharing out of love and concern.

Before reading the letter, I explained that God instructed me to write the letter raw and uncut so that they would be able to see the detrimental things that they missed and the dangers behind it.

The Letter (summarized)

From the moment our family stepped foot in the church, leadership has had eyes on my husband. You saw the call on his life and immediately started trying to help make it come into fruition. He was asked to join multiple teams, and some he joined voluntarily. At one point, he was involved in six different areas. In addition to that, he had been asked to serve in three other areas. While doing all that, he was also volunteering for just about every task requested by the church and our members. He was all in.

The problem was, while doing all of that, everything was being fed but his spirit. He was not growing spiritually. Aside from church activities, he was not seeking God. Instead, he was unknowingly perfecting church culture, behavior, and vernacular. The spirits of legalism and religion attached themselves to him.

Unfortunately, he's still battling them. From the outside, it appeared he was on fire for God (and he thought he was). Internally, the attention he was receiving began to feed his ego. Sadly, he didn't even realize it. He thought that his works equated to relationship with God. He became prideful and arrogant. He stopped valuing his family. He abandoned us. He put everything before us. Through no fault of the church, he was also training for boxing 5-6 days a week. We rarely saw him. The kids and I missed him. I expressed our concerns with him, but he didn't have the mindset to receive them. Our marriage was not in a good place. It was so bad that one evening, I was in severe pain and had to go to the ER. He allowed me to go by myself and chose to go train for boxing. But on several occasions when the church or our members had a need, he dropped everything.

His lines were blurred.

This cycle continued for over two years. Our family was broken.

After those two years (due to some things that he brought to my attention), our marriage suffered an even bigger blow. Things with my husband was way more serious than originally thought.

We have been through a lot since joining the church. Our family has been torn. Through a lot of prayer and therapy, we discovered that the attention my husband was getting was filling childhood voids and feeding years-worth of familiar spirits.

He never pulled back to quit on ministry. He pulled back to heal, get the family right, purify his motives, build relationship with God, and find his identity. He pulled back because he had an issue with allowing himself to be pulled everywhere, by everyone, and not being able to focus on home.

There are still some things he needs to be delivered from, and we are working on them. The man that you guys want, miss, and grew to love was not who God made him to be. You all didn't realize that what you saw was a man hating himself and trying to be the exact opposite. We have been working on healing individually, as a couple, as a family. My husband's relationship with the kids has suffered greatly. He is trying to restore it. We are continuing to work through this. The goal is to help him find identity in himself and Christ; to build a strong foundation in Him.

We have been taking ministry classes online and will be taking Bible-based marriage classes. God has a ministry for us, and this process is a vital part of the development.

Yes, my husband may have gone from a 10 to a 4, but he never stopped reaching out and he never quit on God. God is working on him and has a process. He will be who God called him to be on God's timeline. We are supposed to be obedient to Him, not the church. We are supposed to hear God's voice and instructions for ourselves, not consistently take other people's word for it. We need to be dependent on God, not people. We are supposed to hide prophesy in our heart and let God lead us.

He has not grown to the point where he can hear God's voice. He hasn't developed an unction. How does he know what steps he should be taking if he's not hearing it from God? Shouldn't that be the first step in ministry? Building a true relationship with God, growing in the Spirit, and being led by Him?? Aren't we supposed to "seek ye first the kingdom of God?"

Leadership mentioned last year that they only wanted candidates for the board who are led by the Spirit and can hear from God to help move the church vision forward. Does that not apply to up-and-coming ministers and leaders? Shouldn't it apply to everyone? This is what my husband desires for himself, and he takes it very seriously. Please let him get there. There has been such an urgency to get him to the pulpit, he has been shown ungodly favoritism, has been allowed to cut vital corners, and has not had a chance to grow in Godly character. It doesn't line up with the Word. Instead of helping him, it has severely hindered him.

If the focus isn't on spiritual growth, he will be a minister with no anointing. He doesn't want to be a mascot, but a true minister of God's Word. Every time he gets called out during service, he puts pressure on himself to hurry relationship with God to meet the church's timeline. It makes him feel like a failure.

Over these past four years, my experience has not been as welcoming.

I served for a year and a half, and leadership didn't even know my name. I have experienced being right next to my husband, and him being greeted and me ignored. This has happened several times and has been observed by others. I have been ignored via text and email. I have been greeted with indifference, while my husband has been received enthusiastically.

As I said before, our family has been through a lot over the past few years. I have suffered a tremendous amount of pain and heartache. I have been to the altar various times and have broken completely down. On one of those occasions, a pastor came and laid hands on me and simply said, "stop being so arrogant" before moving on to the next person. I was not sure what that meant but it was hurtful and made me reluctant to ever go to the altar again.

Through the painful season, no one ever reached out to see if I was okay. I broke down often at church and was visibly struggling. No one had eyes to see. The concern and focus have always been on my husband.

In an attempt to help shed light on what I believed may have been an oversight by the church, I asked leadership if the church could consider providing ongoing education, guidance, and support to help leaders learn how to balance ministry and family. I was told, "God knew you had a family when He called you." That has been the undertone of the narrative of the church. That has been the narrative directed toward our family.

God created marriage and family first (in Genesis). It is our first ministry, period. The church is suffering because families are suffering. We are trying to break that cycle, but it seems to bother the leadership.

I don't understand. The kids and I are not keeping him from his purpose. Doesn't the church want men and women of God to be in position in their homes?

In 1 Timothy, it asks how can a man run God's church if he can't manage his own family? It also indicates how a man's prayers can be hindered if he is not doing right by his wife. We can't ignore that. The Word also outlines the expectations of the roles of Overseer and Deacon in the church. Why are we not using that as a guideline? Why are we not checking fruit? There's also a warning against choosing Elders in haste.

Leadership has operated in haste since we stepped foot in the door.

Why? What's the rush? Why go against the Word?

The Word also says that my husband and I are one flesh, so why are we not being treated equally? None of this makes natural sense. 1 Corinthians says that God is not the author of confusion.

We have continued to serve the house faithfully and in love. I mentioned these things in hopes that it will refocus, rebuild, and restore the ministry.

The house has struggled with the anointing because we have been out of order. Chains are not being broken, and yokes are not being destroyed. The culture of the church must change. Families and marriages are broken. Individuals are broken. The focus has been on ministry and not on building up God's people. We need to be strong in the Lord so that we can serve in spirit and truth.

I have been addressing this in prayer for some time. I have been praying for foundational change in the house. It wasn't until recently God urged me to finally speak. He urged me to share all my concerns unfiltered. He allowed me to see that there is a spirit hovering over the house that is in operation. It is hindering the move of God. It's harmful and mimicking the Holy Spirit. I pray the shepherds of the house can identify it, bind it, and get God's house back in order so Holy Spirit will truly be welcome.

The leaders were shocked. They addressed some of what was said and provided explanations. They also apologized for the oversight with my husband and the treatment I experienced. They expressed how they wished we would have shared this sooner. We explained how we felt it was all in God's timing. They asked me about the spirit I mentioned, and I suggested that they pray and ask God to reveal it. We thanked them for their time, and they thanked us for our honesty.

We did it! My husband and I were happy and relieved. I knew in my heart that no matter what the outcome was, we did our part.

FINALE

Though we had the talk with the leaders, I didn't have the level of peace I expected.

I asked the Lord for more clarity and guidance. I started having dreams of an ungodly entity lifting me up, pulling me by my feet. In each dream, I knew the entity wasn't of God. I tried to scream, "Jesus!" but I couldn't. It was as if I was muzzled. After several attempts, I was finally able to scream His name.

One night, I finally had a dream that provided the clarity I'd asked God for.

In the dream, I was in the sanctuary of the church (our actual church). I was sitting on the left side with my Bible, study notebooks, and journals. They were spread out on the seat to my right. As I was sitting, someone from the church came and sat directly in front of me. They didn't speak to me or even look at me. They sat with their back to me. At one point, it looked as if they were going to turn around and say something to me, but instead they got up and sat in the middle of the sanctuary with another person from the church. They both looked at me and started whispering to each other. Immediately a force pulled me out of my seat by my feet. It was pulling me toward the front of the church. Again, I had no control. I knew it was demonic, so I tried calling for Jesus. Again, it was like I was muzzled. After three or four attempts, I was able to scream the name of Jesus. The dream was over.

I woke up with clarity. I knew that God was showing me the demonic activity in the church, where it was coming from, and that I was being targeted. Again, God confirmed that we were not safe and informed me that our spiritual life and death depended on leaving the church. I knew we had shared our concerns with the church hoping for change, but I realized that we weren't meant to stay.

I told my husband about the dream and what it meant. I told him I was being targeted, and that the spiritual life and death of our family depended on leaving the church. I explained how even though we had shared our concerns with the church hoping they would change, we weren't meant to stay. I believed we were only meant to deliver the message as an eye-opener. We discussed everything that we had endured and how unbiblical the churches actions were.

I expressed that I felt uneasy when thinking about the church, and how it felt like my spirit was dying whenever I stepped foot in it. I asked for his input and asked if he'd received anything from God. He said that he hadn't but didn't feel comfortable going back after what I'd shared.

He said, "What kind of husband and father would I be if I continued to allow my family to be in that type of environment?"

Praise the Lord!!!

I knew that this decision was very difficult for my husband because his heart was still very connected to the church. I believe he'd developed a soul tie. I was so proud of him! I finally felt relief.

We informed church leadership of our decision. They expressed how they were sorry to see us go but wished us well.

We attended one last service. Though we'd experienced hardship within the church, there were many people who treated us like family through the years. Afterward, the leader that I had served directly under thanked me for my dedication to the team. I expressed my gratitude and shared what a pleasure it had been to serve throughout the years. The leader asked one of the pastors if they could send me off with prayer. In what seemed to be an indifferent and irritated tone, the reply was "Huh, are YOU gonna do it??", as if it was the last thing on earth anyone would want to do. Like it was a chore, and I wasn't worth praying for. The leader was stunned at the reaction, and so were several other people in the room.

After an awkward silence, the leader prayed for me and my family. I tried to focus on the prayer, but all I could think about is how good God is. I could have been offended by the pastor's reaction, but instead I chuckled inside and thanked the Lord for showing me that we had made the right decision. He loved me enough to send me out the door with one last confirmation. He's so clutch!! Thank you, Lord!!

Full of boldness and joy, I walked out of the door with my head held high and never looked back.

As I indicated earlier, there were many people who treated us like family. We'd developed friendships with people who genuinely loved and supported us. Because we left quietly, no one really knew we were officially gone. People started noticing our absence and began to reach out. We didn't go into detail because we didn't feel it was appropriate at the time. We just told them that we left out of obedience to God.

One day, I received a call from a member that I was close to.

They were calling to check up on us. They weren't aware that we had officially left the church. They thought we were still on a break. I explained how we were being obedient to God, and how he'd shown us some things connected to the church that weren't healthy for our family. The member voiced concern about our departure and indicated that God told them that leaving could hinder the call on my husband's life. They also made a statement that inferred I was getting in the way of his calling and causing spiritual death. I knew that this was the seducing spirit speaking because it was the exact opposite of what God said.

I felt sick for days after the phone call. Eventually I realized that it was the result of a word curse. I don't even think the member realized they were cursing us. They truly felt like they were delivering a word from God out of love. The enemy was trying to seduce us into returning to the church. I prayed, fasted, and pulled that word out by the root. I had the feeling God had something else to tell me. I pressed in for an answer.

God kept pointing me to two scriptures.

As soon as they had brought them out, one of them said, "Flee for your lives! Don't look back, and don't stop anywhere in the plain! Flee to the mountains or you will be swept away!

Genesis 19:17 (NIV)

The LORD said to Abram, "Go from your country, your people and your father's household to the land I will show you.

Genesis 12:1 (NIV)

In addition to the scriptures, I had another dream. I was in our actual bedroom, and a member of the church came in and tried to seduce me. I woke up and knew exactly what it meant.

Not only did God want us to leave the church. He wanted us to separate from it completely. I had learned early on about the power of ministry agreement. God brought it to my remembrance. He showed me that as powerful as it is when used for good, it is just as powerful when used for bad. The devil used the agreement to push his agenda. He showed me that as long as the seducing spirit is hovering over the church and is tolerated, everyone in the church is in agreement with it, whether they knew it or not. If we weren't careful, the spirit could seduce us into going back to the church to be under its influence.

As God said before, this was all a matter of spiritual life and death. We had to distance ourselves completely.

I told my husband what God had shown me. He wasn't ready for it. He didn't like it or agree, and I didn't expect him to. This was a lot for him, and leaving the church was hard enough. I didn't press the issue, but I started being intentional in distancing myself. This was difficult because we'd been close to these people for years and couldn't fully disclose the reason for the distance. I didn't stop communicating completely, I just lessened it consistently over time.

My husband was having a hard time. He had been connected to a group within the church that he'd grown extremely close to. He had told them that we left the church under God's instruction, but he was still a part of the chat. I knew that the longer he stayed connected, he was more likely to be seduced. I told him to be careful.

Within a month or two, my husband found himself being pulled back in. Though he was no longer a church member, they had given him an open invitation to go on fellowship outings and to serve at community events with them. My husband accepted. Before acting on any of them, he realized that he was allowing himself to be sucked back in. It was as if he was still a member of the church. He admitted to the group that he wasn't being fully obedient to God's instructions, and kindly asked to be removed from the chat. I knew it was a difficult decision. I was so proud of him!

We were completely disconnected.

THE AFTERMATH

Everything that led up to leaving the church was so dramatic. It was like a never-ending crescendo, with the climax being the moment we separated from the church.

Then there was silence.

We were finally in a place where we could focus on our marriage and family without distractions. Without all the noise, we were left with just us. Sadly, we had no idea what that looked like. It felt like we had been dragged through a crazy portal and were just dropped off on the other side. The battle was over, but there was still fighting to do. This experience had changed us all; my husband, me, and the kids. We were unrecognizable. We were all wounded.

My husband was so confused and had no sense of identity. He didn't know who he was naturally or in Christ. He didn't know how to be himself. The only way he knew how to pursue Christ was through works. Without the works, he felt extremely lost. He didn't comprehend the value of being still and equated it to wasting time. It was as if he wanted to skip relationship, healing, and deliverance and fast forward straight to his purpose. He was anxious, frustrated, angry, and impatient. Communication with him was difficult and unnatural. Almost everything that came out of his mouth was grandiose. It seemed he couldn't answer a simple question without preaching. The kids were frustrated because they felt as though they couldn't talk to him. Basic conversation would turn into sermons. They would ask him questions that wouldn't get answered because he would go off on tangents. It seemed that if it wasn't about church, he didn't know what to say. His heart was broken because he realized he didn't know his own children or how to interact naturally with them. It was like they were strangers. He expressed not knowing how to genuinely interact with anyone. He was still having issues hearing God's voice and began to grow weary. There were no works to fall back on. He was extremely broken, and his mind was all over the place. His identity was wrapped up in ministry and not Christ. Now that we had separated, he felt useless and lost.

He had been Churtched.

I too was having issues. I was in relationship with God and knew for sure that he loved me, but I still felt less than. I felt alone with no one to talk to. I didn't feel like I mattered to people, and I didn't feel like I had a clear purpose. I had been in battle mode so long, I never allowed myself time to feel and address the hurt. I hadn't fully dealt with the pain of my husband's actions, nor did I recognize how hurtful the treatment from the church really was. Bitterness, resentment, and unforgiveness were hidden in my heart and were slowly poisoning my soul. In the midst of it all, I had allowed the church experience to affect the way I saw myself. Watching my husband's purpose be called out so many times over the years with no word about mine started messing with my mind. I realize that I too had started to idolize the church. I was looking for their validation instead of God's.

I was Churtched.

Our children developed resentment toward church and us. They resented church because, for over four years, we allowed it to take over our lives. On average, we were at church or involved in church activities three or four days a week (sometimes five). We didn't balance it well (at all). We didn't spend enough quality time together outside of church.

Our youngest child expressed early on feeling as if there was no life outside of church, and that we were being brainwashed. They were estranged from my husband and not too happy with me either.

After leaving the church, we started worship, community service and bible study on Sundays as a family. The kids did not receive it well. We realized that they hated every moment of it and didn't want to hear anything about God. It was heartbreaking to see how two once-smiling kids had turned so cold. When we first started going to church, they were genuinely happy, excited to go and eager to learn about God. We didn't steward them well. We had unknowing misrepresented God and they had formed their own opinion about Him.

Due to our negligence, they had been Churtched.

The condition of our marriage wasn't any better. We hadn't consistently taken time to work on healing because we were so wrapped up in church affairs. We were in survival mode. The events had driven a bit of a wedge between us, and we were in a weird place. I had developed a poor self-image while questioning whether God really ordained me to be my husband's wife. Ironically, I just didn't feel worthy. It didn't make sense given all the fighting I did on his behalf.

He was still struggling with identity, relationship, and priorities. It was a mess. We still loved each other, but we'd allowed the flame to burn out.

We had allowed our marriage to be Churtched.

GOD IS GOOD

M y all-time favorite Bible story is Joseph's.

Though my experience is minimal in comparison to his, I've felt a connection with the emotions he must have been feeling being thrown in a pit by the ones he loved, sold off to strangers, accused of a crime he didn't commit, thrown in prison, and forgotten. I'm sure he experienced a range of emotions: betrayal, worthlessness, anger, rejection, insignificance and loneliness. I also felt all those things.

Despite all the heartache, Joseph never lost sight of God. He never forgot the things promised to him. He stayed faithful and never compromised. Though enduring years of pain, he triumphed to the happy ending. God exalted him and put him in a position to save the lives of many, including the people who hurt him the most, his brothers. The best part of the story is his display of compassion and forgiveness toward them. His brothers humbly stood before him in need, riddled with fear (and maybe guilt and shame). Joseph could have reacted in response to the way they had treated him but instead he gave them these words of comfort and reassurance: "You intended to harm me, but God intended it for good to accomplish what is now being done, the saving of many lives" (Genesis 50:20, NIV).

Yes, my experience was painful, and I felt many emotions. Just like Joseph, I never lost sight of God. I leaned on Him like never before. I believe that I, too, have been exalted by God, and what the devil meant for evil God is using for good to accomplish the saving of many churches and souls through this testimony.

Years ago, during the most difficult time, God put it on my heart to start journaling. I was having a hard time expressing my emotions, and my prayer life had fallen under attack. I began writing down my thoughts and prayers. Who knew that God would use the journaling to build me up to be a writer?! "And we know that in all things God works for the good of those who love Him, who have been called according to His purpose" (Romans 8:28, NIV).

In the introduction, I shared my first encounter with the Holy Spirit. At the touch of an unknown pastor's hand, I received a tangible filling. Decades later, I believe it played a role in my deliverance. I had no idea what it meant to consecrate, and somehow, I did it for 6 months. I knew what I wanted and needed from God and what was necessary to obtain it. I didn't receive advice or instruction from any man. I believe it was the leading of the Holy Spirit.

Not only was the six months a period of consecration, but it was also a time of training and building. I learned how to press in and operate in expectation. I learned how to live a life of worship to our Lord. I presented my body as a "living sacrifice, holy and pleasing to God" (Romans 12:1, NIV). It laid the foundation of my faith.

Afterward, I received a fresh filling of the Holy Spirit and the activation of spiritual gifts. At the time, I had no idea what any of this meant, nor did I care. I just wanted to continue to grow closer to our Lord. I thank the Lord for the ignorance because my motives may not have been as pure. The Lord was undoubtedly with me. I had a supernatural strength, grace, and endurance. The events with the church and my husband may have broken my heart but it didn't break ME. The news about my husband's behavior at work was painful, but it didn't destroy me. The Holy Spirit was standing in the gap.

God is Good!

Some years have passed, and our family is still intact. We did whatever was necessary to keep us together (therapy, wise council, deliverance, etc.). I am still free from depression and suicidal ideation. My kidney condition has not progressed. Daily, I still strive to worship and glorify the Lord in everything I do as He continues to reveal his purpose for my life.

My husband is still pursuing relationship with God and allowing Him to unlock identity and purpose. He values his family and will never forget that we are his first ministry. We value our marriage and keep it a priority. We are back in church and strive to maintain a healthy church/life balance. Our past experience never robbed us of the desire to go to church because we left no doors open for resentment and bitterness. The Word says not to forsake the assembly (Hebrews 10:25, KJV), and we stand on that. We love God and desire to stay in his will. We were patient and wise in finding a new house of worship. It's a completely different experience, and it has blessed us. The Holy Spirit moves freely, and the religious spirit is not welcome.

It's been a long journey, and we still a have a long way to go. We know that we are not perfect, but we know who is: Jesus Christ our Lord and Savior. "Such confidence we have through Christ before God. Not that we are competent in ourselves to claim anything for ourselves, but our competence comes from God" (2 Corinthians 3:4-5, NIV).

HINDSIGHT IS 2020

Many lessons were learned from this experience with the church. It's true what the Word says in Romans 8:28 (NIV), "And we know that in all things God works for the good of those who love Him, who have been called according to His purpose." It was difficult, painful, and traumatic, but we made it through victorious. We have battle scars that marked us for life. We gained wisdom that you can't get without having been through a great trial. My prayer life was activated. I developed a hunger for the Word and fasting. I learned how to press in, lean on God and hear His voice. He spoke to me ever so clearly. He gave me strength to endure and preserved me. I was living a crash course in warfare and the discerning of spirits. I learned how cunning the enemy is and witnessed how he can use a church to distract God's people and hinder (even destroy) relationship with Him. He showed me how church, purpose, and calling can become idols. I thank the Lord for this experience.

With the wisdom I gained, I can now educate His people.

The New Christian/Congregant

Be careful not to join a church too quickly.

Don't allow your emotions to lead you to a hasty decision.

Don't be distracted by gifts and entertainment. Spend time as a visitor for a while. Ask yourselves, "Do the sermons line up with the Bible? Are you learning anything?"

For a new Christian, these things can be difficult to discern. Take time to study what was discussed during service at home by comparing it with the Bible. Purchase a Bible that breaks the material down in a way you can understand. Allow time to observe fruit (good or bad).

This is one of the most important decisions you will make in life. Committing to a church is allowing people access to your soul. Ask God for direction in joining the church. If you get the green light, get to know the people around you. If the ministry isn't leading you deeper into relationship with Jesus, it's a red flag. Don't ignore red flags. Don't allow yourself to be rushed or pressured into anything.

Always be mindful of church/life balance. If you're married, your marriage is your first ministry. If you're married with kids, your family is your first ministry. Stand firm on that. Above all, "Seek ye first the kingdom of God, and his righteousness; and all these things shall be added unto you" (Matthew 6:33, KJV).

Church Leadership

Take time to get to know new congregants.

Don't start prophesying as soon as they walk through the door. You may see a gifting or a calling on someone, but take time to observe their fruit and foundation in Jesus before calling it out. Relationship with God should be the first thing you lead your congregants to. If God calls one family member, he calls them all. They may not all be called to be pastors, but they all need to be strong in the Lord so that they can have the ability to endure the weight of ministry as a unit.

Strong families build strong churches.

Focus on building men and women of God who know how to steward their families with excellence. Don't favor certain gifts over others. The body needs all its members to operate effectively.

Don't overlook the need for deliverance and don't push people into leadership positions who are still in major need of it. Gifts and talents don't break chains or destroy yokes. This type of environment invites demons and allows them to be comfortable. Teach and encourage congregants how to discern the voice of God for themselves so that pastors don't become their god. "He must increase, we must decrease" (John 3:30, KJV).

Take Responsibility

Though this book outlines our experience with the church, it goes much deeper. The Word says to "be alert and of sober mind" because "your enemy the devil prowls around like a roaring lion looking for someone to devour" (1 Peter 5:8, NIV). It also says that "every man is tempted, when he is drawn away of his own lust, and enticed" (James 1:14, KJV).

We were not sober-minded. We were so excited about our decision to finally commit to our lives to Christ, we dove in headfirst. Our hearts were in the right place, but we weren't wise. We allowed ourselves to be led by our emotions. The devil was waiting to devour us. The easiest way for him to get in is through open doors.

An open door is a compromise within your soul that allows access to the devil and his demons. They can be caused by sin, unresolved trauma, pain or unforgiveness (just to name a few). My husband and I had open doors, and the devil walked right in. Open doors can also fuel lusts. Demons have desires that get carried out through you. Temptations are presented according to these lusts.

These are the things we walked in the door of the church with, and for that we cannot place blame. As adults we must take responsibility for our own healing and "work out our own salvation with fear and trembling" (Philippians 2:12, KJV).

Hidden

I mentioned in a previous chapter how the experience left me feeling less-than and unimportant. For years, I fought a silent battle. The times I cried out at the altar was a cry for help from God and the people around me. I didn't want much, just the shoulder of someone who cared to cry on. No one really knew what I was going through because I felt I was sworn to secrecy. For a while, I didn't understand what was going on. I thought something was wrong with me. I thought I was crazy and even started to pity myself.

As the years have passed, I realized that a lot of what I perceived as being looked over and ignored, was really God hiding me. He buried me like a seed for protection, nourishment, and growth. It was part of my process. There were some things within me that God had to pull out. As my husband was in the spotlight, I was in the secret place building relationship with Jesus. I'm grateful that I wasn't in the spotlight. My spiritual growth was consistent, and I didn't have any outside pressure. I persevered through the suffering, and it built up my character (Romans 5:3-4, NIV). I experienced self-deliverance, enhanced discernment, gift activation, and the pure love of God. I spent quality time in his Word, prayer, and in worship. I developed a lifestyle of worship so strong I learned to see the enemy coming.

Even now my dependence on Him is vital. I have to stay in

close proximity to Him, or I don't do well. "He is the Vine, and I am a branch, apart from Him I can do nothing" (John 15:5, NIV). I thank the Lord for the time He kept me hidden. It shaped me, healed me, and set me free.

The Seducing Spirit

As mentioned previously, seducing spirits aim to lure us away from God's will for our lives. It creates false signs and wonders to deceive you into thinking that what you are pursuing is Godly. It operates in flattery and tricks you into thinking that you've arrived spiritually.

This spirit had my husband. All his weaknesses were exploited and used as bait for the lusts he fell into. The voids from childhood that made him feel worthless and invisible made him easy to seduce. An atmosphere was orchestrated that made my husband feel good about himself; meanwhile, seduction was using the open doors in his soul to plant lust, pride, and religion. His flesh overpowered him because his spirit was weak. There was little to no room for the Holy Spirit to move. He had been seduced into rebellion while believing he was walking in the will of God.

Seduction is a sneaky liar that looks and sounds good but is of the devil. The wounded, desperate, and immature are its prey. The subtle way it operates is dangerous, so we must stay alert, sober-minded and humble.

So again: "Be alert and of sober mind. Your enemy the devil prowls around like a roaring lion looking for someone to devour" (1 Peter 5:8, NIV). Also, "Do not think of yourself more highly than you ought, but rather think of yourself with sober judgement, in accordance with the faith God has distributed to each of you" (Romans 12:3, NIV).

The Religious Spirit

This experience taught me how cunning the devil is. He used the church against itself by infiltrating the system and watering it down. He seduces church goers away from Jesus by occupying them with the work of the ministry. He creates false signs and wonders to create the illusion of the Holy Spirit. People are drawn more by the church experience than the Holy Spirit. Gifts, talents, and charisma are valued more than the anointing. People show up to be wooed by emotion and entertainment. Church leaders become puffed up with pride because they are looking at church attendance through natural eyes. Souls become less of a priority.

This creates a scenario where people are struggling with sin and not understanding why. They start checking off boxes to make sure they are doing x, y, and z, not realizing that God is not in the list. To hide the fact that they are struggling they create a perfection-driven, overly religious facade like the Pharisees. Instead of developing in the Holy Spirit, they develop a "form of godliness" (2 Timothy 3:5, NIV). They feel lost, condemned, and grow weary.

They have unknowingly taken on the religious spirit. This spirit wreaks havoc. It takes over and opens the door to other spirits. Now the church is full of depressed, suicidal, adulterous, judgmental, and deceitful people who are stuck in a cycle of condemnation and are ashamed to admit that they are struggling. Despite the torment, they continue to dedicate themselves to the show that they call church.

This is one of the spirits that attached itself to my husband and appears to have caused the most damage. It tainted his God-given identity, delayed purpose, and distorted his perception of what relationship with Jesus looks like in his life. It created a works-based salvation, in which he feels he can't work hard enough to please

Jesus. He, too, has been stuck in the cycle of condemnation. It has caused him so much confusion and heartache.

I do not wish this spirit upon anyone.

Prophecy

In the beautiful words of one of my mentors, Apostle Deborah Edwards (DREEMM, Cincinnati), "Prophecy is the revelation of heavenly things released into the earth for the manifestation of God's glory and fulfillment of His will." It's what God has already spoken over your life.

Prophecy is a supernatural gift that is mesmerizing. It is made to strengthen, encourage, and comfort (1 Corinthians 14:3). Unfortunately, it also has the ability to stir up emotions due to spiritual immaturity and may cause people to act on them.

When a word of prophecy is released over you, it should be practical as it applies to your life, line up with the word, and confirm what God has already put in your heart. Some words are for the now, some are for the near future, and some are for the distant future. When we hear a word, it is up to us to hide it in our heart and take it to God for further instruction.

Out of immaturity and desperation, many Christians hear a word and act on it right away. They labor and toil to try to make it come to pass. We must wait on God's timing. "Time has to catch up to God's Word" (one of my favorite quotes from my mentor, Pastor L. Shakir). God operates outside of time, so we may receive a word today that's meant for 30 years in the future.

Wait patiently on the Lord and build yourself up in the Word.

There's nothing wrong with preparing yourself for the word God has spoken over your life; just be careful that you are not rush-

73

ing God or manipulating situations to assist certain things in falling into place. This is a form of witchcraft. It's dangerous and can delay or destroy God's plan in your life.

He gives us free will, but we should not abuse it. I have found that when you hide prophecy in your heart and stay focused on the Lord, you'll find yourself walking in the fulfillment of a prophecy without realizing it. It has been my experience time and time again, including the writing of this book. It was prophesied to me a few years ago. I didn't realize that this book was the fulfillment until I was in the middle of writing it!

Be patient and trust God!

Write down the revelation and make it plain on tablets so that a herald may run with it. For the revelation awaits an appointed time; it speaks of the end and will not prove false. Though it linger, wait for it; it will certainly come and will not delay.

Habakkuk 2:2-3, NIV

It Starts at Home

Train up a child in the way he should go, and when he is old he will not depart from it.

Proverbs 22:6, KJV

We spent all those years in church not knowing we were hurting our children. As I mentioned, we did not have a healthy church/life balance. We showed our children church but failed to show them Jesus. We weren't living wicked lives at home, but we weren't nurturing them spiritually. We weren't praying as a family (other than saying grace), and we didn't present the word. We left it up to the church.

Just as we don't want our children learning morals and fundamentals at school, the same should go for church. As parents, we have a responsibility to help build a Godly foundation in our children's lives so that they can be in all environments and have the ability to discern the truth from a lie, whether it be in the world or in a church.

Not Every Church is the Correct Fit

Not every church is the correct fit.

Jesus realized this in Luke 4:24 (NIV). He said, "no prophet is accepted in his hometown." He was in an environment where the people were so familiar with Him that they didn't realize who He was. They saw Him as common and didn't have the faith to receive his miracles.

The same goes for us. Not every church is going to recognize the giftings that God has put within you, and not every church can develop those gifts. This is perfectly normal, and it is okay. As people operate in different giftings, so do churches.

Some churches may operate more in the evangelical, and some may operate more in the prophetic. As you develop more in the Lord, you will know what environments feed your spirit. If you are sitting in a church that isn't helping you grow or develop in your gifting, ask God for direction. He may lead you to leave the current church and direct you toward a new one that has the tools to develop you. He also may instruct you to stay and send mentors to help you grow or use the opportunity for you to serve and receive direct teaching from the Holy Spirit.

There may also be instances where a church does not welcome

or receive you. If you know you have maintained the right heart, motives, and conducted yourself in an orderly fashion, God may have you leave, "shake the dust off of your feet," and take your peace with you (Matthew 10:13-14, KJV).

We should never stay in a situation that is causing turmoil or stagnancy without asking God for direction.

Work Out Your Own Salvation

It is extremely important as Christians to work out our own salvation (Philippians 2:12, KJV).

Yes, the church may have missed the mark in leading us as newly dedicated Christians into relationship with Jesus, but after a certain point, it was up to us. We all must have the desire to seek Him for ourselves. Going to church every Sunday to get a word from the pastor is not enough. It's spiritual starvation. Church leaders are there to guide us, not to replace God.

It's vital to keep God on the throne in our lives. The COVID-19 shut down is a perfect example of what happens when you go to church every Sunday and participate in church activities without growing in relationship with God. You can be in church seven days a week and still not know Him. When the churches shut down, many people failed to return. Some fell back into sin. Sadly, I believe that many were probably in sin all along or didn't have true victory over it. Attending church distracted them enough and made them feel guilty enough to quell it temporarily.

When you have relationship with Jesus, and He's truly the Lord over your life, you look to Him to hold you accountable. He will give you the conviction, strength, and deliverance you need to turn away from the sin you battle with. When He is Lord over your life, natural circumstances will not dictate your pursuit. The altar of our heart has no fixed location, and the Bible is portable. We have no excuse. Our bodies are temples that house the Holy Spirit, we must build ourselves up with firm foundations. "Unless the LORD builds the house, the builders labor in vain" (Psalm 127:1, NIV).

We have been so focused and dependent on the church house, but WE ARE THE CHURCH. It's time to get in position!!

A LETTER TO THE CHURTCHED

Brothers and Sisters,

I know the experience you went through was painful. I know that you felt used, abused, and even worthless. I know the experience may have left you bitter, offended, full of resentment, and confused. Remember that "God is not the author of confusion" (1 Corinthians 14:33, KJV).

Though God does not cause pain, He sometimes allows it. "And we know that in all things God works for the good of those who love Him, who have been called according to His purpose" (Romans 8:28, NIV). I know your heart is broken but "the LORD is near to the brokenhearted and saves the crushed in spirit" (Psalm 34:18, ESV). He will 'heal your broken heart and bandage your wounds' (Psalm 147:3, NLT).

Brothers and Sisters, "stand firm to the end" (Matthew 24:13, NIV).

Consider it pure joy, my brothers and sisters, whenever you face trials of many kinds, because you know that the testing of your faith produces perseverance. Let perseverance finish its work so that you may be mature and complete, not lacking anything.

James 1:2-4, NIV

The pain you experienced was as a result of broken people. God was not in it. Please be very careful not to confuse the two. Find it in your heart to forgive. "Love your enemies and pray for those who persecute you" (Matthew 5:44, NIV). Do not allow the experience to cause you to stumble. "If your right hand causes you to stumble, cut it off and throw it away. It is better for you to lose one part of your body than for your whole body to go to hell" (Matthew 5:30, NIV). Do not harbor offense because it will harden your heart and hinder the flow of God's love through you. "A brother offended is harder to be won than a strong city: And their contentions are like the bars of a castle" (Proverbs 18:19, KJV).

Yes, the assembly is important, but our primary focus should be on Jesus. He is the Bridegroom expecting a holy and blameless bride (Ephesians 5:27, NIV). He will not entertain excuses regarding how the church or other people prevented us from seeking Him and having a repentant heart.

Family, if church hurt is affecting your walk, seek healing. Ask the Lord to heal you. He wants you healed.

If you're having difficulty, find a seasoned man or woman of God that you trust for guidance and/or find a deliverance ministry. Time is short. We don't have time to continue to carry weight that could possibly keep us here on earth when Jesus calls us to meet Him up in the clouds.

Press through and continue to work out your own salvation with fear and trembling (Philippians 2:12, KJV). The Lord loves us and is very patient with our process. He doesn't want any of us to perish, but everyone to come to repentance (2 Peter 3:9, NIV).

Don't give up! Fight the good fight, finish the race and keep the faith (2 Timothy 4:7, NIV).

God bless you all!

EPILOGUE: GENESIS 12:1

The Lord said to Abram, "Go from your country, your people and your father's household to the land I will show you...."

Genesis 12:1 (NIV)

The word we received from God in The Finale through Genesis 12:1 was much deeper than leaving the church. It was a prophetic word that changed our lives. Not only did God want us to leave the church. He was instructing us to leave everything and everyone we knew to go to a foreign land. He revealed the location through His Word and our would-be new home in a dream. He even had a church for us!!! He was so specific!!

Within five months, we had sold our old house, bought a new one in the new location, packed up all our belongings, and relocated to the new land. We left jobs and people behind. God wanted us to start over and didn't want us bringing anyone or anything with us that didn't serve the purpose He had for us in the new land. He showed me that this was a Psalm 23 move! He wanted us to rest, recover, and allow Him to prepare us for the journey ahead.

Within a year we started building a Kingdom business. God

made it clear that it wasn't His will for us to work traditional jobs. He led us to get rid of any and everything that got in the way of our pursuit of Him.

Our life is our worship to Him, and it is also our ministry. There is no separation between the two. As I mentioned in Hindsight is 2020, WE ARE THE CHURCH! Spreading the good news starts with ourselves, marriages, and families. We carry the message of Christ within us wherever we go. His level of presence in our lives is evident in our lifestyles and reactions.

Let's represent Him well!

ABOUT THE AUTHOR

Tiffani is a God-fearing wife and mother of two who loves to write and create. She loves sunny days, nature, and talking to God while on morning walks. She loves worshipping God not only in song, but with her life. During the first wave of COVID, she discovered a passion (and possibly an anointing) to write and sing songs of the Lord. Through her experience with the church, she discovered a deep burden to help others learn how to develop an authentic and deep relationship with God. Having been delivered from the spirit of depression through intense consecration, fasting, and pursuit, she desires to help others be set free from anything and everything hindering their walk. Her desire for the Lord and His Word grows every day and her heart's desire is to operate at the feet of Jesus. Four of her favorite scriptures are:

> Through Him all things were made; without Him nothing was made that has been made.
>
> John 1:3 (NIV)

> I am the vine; you are the branches. If you remain in me and I in you, you will bear much fruit: apart from me you can do nothing.
>
> John 15:5 (NIV)

I say to the LORD, "You are my Lord; apart from you I have no good thing."

Psalm 16:2 (NIV)

Such confidence we have through Christ before God. Not that we are competent in ourselves to claim anything for ourselves, but our competence comes from God.

2 Corinthians 3:4-5 (NIV)

These scriptures keep her humble and remind her that without Christ there is nothing, she is nothing and can do nothing!

CPSIA information can be obtained
at www.ICGtesting.com
Printed in the USA
BVHW032308091022
649053BV00012B/259